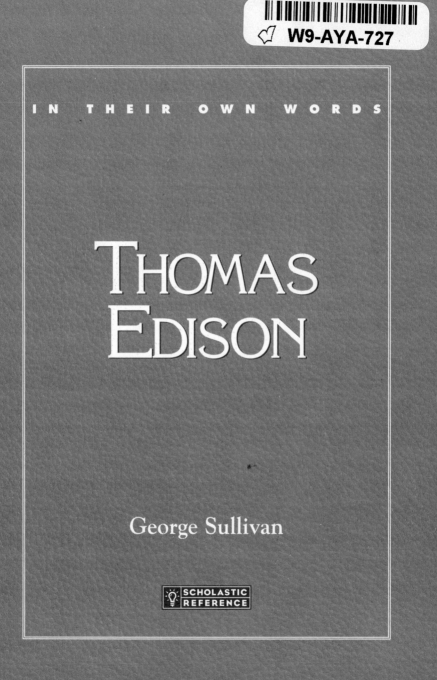

IN THEIR OWN WORDS

THOMAS EDISON

George Sullivan

SCHOLASTIC
REFERENCE

LIBRARY OF CONGRESS CATALOGING-IN-PUBLICATION DATA

Sullivan, George, 1927–
Thomas Edison/George Sullivan.
p.   cm.—(In their own words)
Includes bibliographical references and index.
1. Edison, Thomas, 1847–1931—Juvenile literature.   2. Electric engineers—United
States—Biography—Juvenile literature.   3. Inventors—United States—Biography—
Juvenile literature.   [1. Edison, Thomas A. (Thomas Alva), 1847–1931.   2. Inventors.]
I. Title.   II. In their own words (Scholastic)
TK140.E3 S85 2002
621.3′092—dc21
[B]   2001020727

ISBN 0-439-26319-0

10 9 8 7 6   03 04 05

Composition by Brad Walrod
Printed in the U.S.A.   40
First printing, September 2001

CONTENTS

INTRODUCTION

"I FIND OUT WHAT THE WORLD NEEDS. Then I go ahead and try to invent it."

These are the words of Thomas Alva Edison. They help to explain why he is the greatest inventor in American history. Edison's inventions changed the world.

Edison amazed people with the first practical electric lightbulb. The phonograph was another of his successes. He invented a movie camera and projector, and was one of the first people to produce movies.

Edison also did much more. He invented the business of inventing. He brought together teams of scientists and engineers. He used them to solve problems. In so doing, Edison introduced the idea of the modern research laboratory, which many companies use today.

To Edison, the people who worked for him were "muckers." He called himself the chief mucker. Muck is often defined as mud or filth. A mucker is a person of the lowest rank.

In using these words to describe himself and his coworkers, Edison was telling people that inventing was often hard and messy. Throughout his life, Edison valued hard work. He worked day and night on his projects. He wanted other people to work hard, too.

"Genius," Edison said, "is one percent inspiration and ninety-nine percent perspiration."

Edison was a successful inventor despite a physical challenge. He suffered a hearing loss as a young boy. His hearing became worse as he grew older. But Edison would not let his poor hearing hold him back. He claimed it even worked to his benefit. He wasn't easily distracted, he said, because he heard fewer sounds than other people did. He could concentrate better.

Edison in 1881 at the age of thirty-four. He had already been granted several hundred patents for inventions that had sprung from his creative mind.

Hundreds of books have been written about Thomas Edison. Thousands of articles about him have appeared in newspapers and magazines.

Edison also left behind hundreds of laboratory notebooks. These are filled with his drawings and his comments about his inventions.

There are mountains of business records, too. More than five million pages of written material about Edison are available for study.

Much of this information takes the form of primary sources. Historians use both primary sources and secondary sources to learn about an event or a person of the past.

Primary sources are actual records that have been handed down from a previous time. Letters, diaries, and speeches are primary sources. Newspapers and magazines of the time are primary sources, too.

Edison's patents are another valuable primary source. The government awards patents for new and useful machines or processes. A patent gives a person the right to exclude others from making and selling his or her invention.

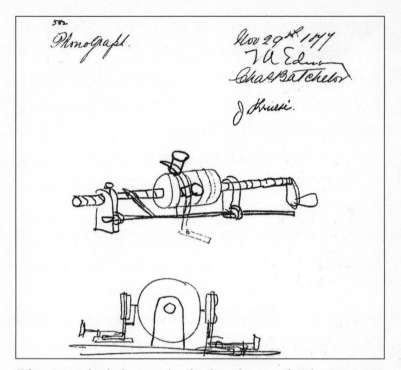

Edison's notebook drawing for the first phonograph. The instrument recorded sound on a rotating metal cylinder covered with tinfoil.

During his lifetime, Edison was granted 1,093 patents in the United States. That's the greatest number ever issued to one person. Edison's patent drawings and his words describing the inventions are highly prized by historians, people who study the past.

Other kinds of primary sources are well known. A

birth certificate is a primary source. A marriage license is a primary source, too.

A secondary source is an indirect or secondhand source. It is the description of an event by someone who did not actually witness it.

A history textbook is a secondary source. So are encyclopedias. Modern books or articles about Edison are secondary sources, too.

Thomas Edison was honest and thrifty. He was confident and seldom gloomy. He saw the good side of things. For example, in December 1914, a fire broke out at Edison's factory buildings in West Orange, New Jersey. Tanks of chemicals in the buildings sent up towering flames. Firefighters had trouble putting out the fire because there was not enough water pressure.

Edison, then sixty-seven years old, stood and watched the blaze. His arms were folded across his chest. His face was calm. He spoke to his son Charles. "Where's Mother?" he asked. "Get her over here. Her friends, too. They'll never see a fire like this again."

On the day after the fire, Edison was a bundle of energy. He directed a crew of more than 1,000 men as they cleared away the debris.

Edison rented factory space in nearby towns. Machines were quickly installed. People were put back to work. Rebuilding began without delay.

Edison expressed how he felt in a newspaper of the day. "I am sixty-seven," he said. "But I'm not too old to make a fresh start."

Edison's confidence was clear. Within a few months, he had his factories operating again.

As these paragraphs suggest, primary sources give us important clues about people. They can help us become aware of what a person might be thinking or feeling. They can help us to understand what a person is truly like.

This book is a secondary source. But it makes use of primary sources. It draws upon the story of Edison's life that he helped to write. It makes use of his laboratory notes, business records, and other personal papers. In so doing, it seeks to tell the real story of Thomas Edison and his many remarkable achievements.

GROWING UP

"THE HAPPIEST TIME OF MY LIFE," Edison once said, "was when I was twelve years old. I was just old enough to have a good time in the world, but not old enough to understand any of its troubles."

Thomas Alva Edison was born on February 11, 1847, in Milan, Ohio. He was the youngest of seven children.

He was named Thomas after one of his uncles. The name Alva was that of a family friend.

Thomas Alva's father, Samuel Edison, was born in Canada. But he opposed the Royal Canadian Government. He joined a rebel movement to fight them. When the government put down the rebellion, Canadian soldiers went looking for him.

Thomas Alva Edison was born in this plain brick house in Milan, Ohio, on February 11, 1847.

So, Sam Edison fled across the border into the United States. He crossed through Michigan and settled in northern Ohio. He then sent for his wife, Nancy, and their children. Thomas Alva was born eight years later.

Sam Edison eventually came to own a mill that made roof shingles in Milan, Ohio, a town of less than 1,000 people. Although it was not big, Milan was a bustling community. A three-mile canal linked

Milan to the Huron River. The river flowed into Lake Erie, one of the Great Lakes.

Each day, hundreds of ox-drawn carts piled high with wheat arrived in Milan. The grain was loaded on barges and into ships bound for ports on the Great Lakes. During the 1840s, Milan was one of the nation's leading grain-shipping ports.

The town was always busy. More than a dozen grain warehouses lined the canal. Milan had its own brewery and a large flour mill. Iron forges and blacksmith shops were common.

There was much to do as a young boy. In the summer, Tom and his friends swam and fished in the canal. In the winter, they skated.

Tom, who was called Al or Alva by his family and friends, was a boy filled with curiosity. He was always asking questions. "Why does a goose squat on the eggs?" he once asked his mother.

"To keep them warm," she answered.

"Why does she keep them warm?"

"So they will hatch."

"What's 'hatch'?"

"It means letting the little geese come out of the shells. They are born that way."

Later that day, Tom was nowhere to be found. His father finally spotted him in a neighbor's barn. He was sitting on a nest of goose eggs and chicken eggs. He was trying to get them to hatch. When they did not, he was disappointed.

Sometimes Tom's desire to learn proved troublesome. When he was six, he started a fire in his father's barn. The flames got out of control, and the barn burned to the ground. Tom received a sound thrashing. He later explained that he wanted to "just see what it would do."

Tom's mother spanked him across the legs when he

The earliest known photo of Thomas Edison, taken when he was four years old.

disobeyed—which was often. Edison once recalled that she always had her birch switch handy. He said that it had "the bark worn off."

Tom once tumbled into the canal and almost drowned. Another time, he fell into a grain elevator. He came out gasping for breath. He had nearly suffocated.

Beginning in about 1853, Milan fell on hard times. The arrival of railroads across the country caused the town's decline. Farmers learned that it was cheaper to ship grain by rail instead of by boat. Milan had no railroad depot, and so the town's economy began to slow down. Sam Edison could not prevent his lumber business from edging toward failure. He decided the family should move.

In the spring of 1854, the Edisons resettled in Port Huron, Michigan. There, Sam Edison rented a comfortable two-story house. It had twelve rooms. Through the big windows there were views of Lake Huron and the nearby St. Clair River.

Not long after the Edisons arrived in Port Huron, Tom fell ill with scarlet fever. He had a sore throat and a high fever. A red rash covered his body. It took Tom a long time to recover. He did not go to school that year. It is believed that the illness may have caused him to suffer a partial loss of hearing.

The next year, Tom was sent off to school for the first time. It was a private school. He later attended public school. Public or private, it didn't matter. Tom did poorly in both.

In those days, students learned lessons by memorizing them. Tom had no patience for such a system. He was curious. He wanted to learn. But he wanted to be able to find out things on his own.

"I remember I [was] never...able to get along at school," he would later write. "I was always at the foot of the class. I used to feel that teachers did not sympathize with me...."

One day, Tom happened to overhear the schoolmaster describe him as being "addled." Tom knew the definition of that word. It meant mixed up or confused. Tom was furious. He stormed out of the classroom. At home, he vowed he would never return to school. He never did. His mother took

Nancy Elliott Edison and Sam Edison chose to homeschool their son Thomas.

him out of the school, and began teaching him at home.

Nancy Edison was well prepared for the task. She had once been a schoolteacher. Besides, she loved her young son very much. Three of her other young children had died. Three of the older children had married and gone out into the world. Tom was the only child left at home. Mrs. Edison enjoyed the time that she and Tom spent together.

Mrs. Edison believed that Tom was a smart boy. She read the stories of Charles Dickens to him. She made him familiar with the plays of William Shakespeare. By the time Tom was nine, he was a rapid reader.

One of the books he read was an elementary science textbook. It was titled *Natural Philosophy*. Edison later said it was "the first book of science I read when [I was] a boy, nine years old, the first I could understand."

The book described a number of chemical experiments. Tom tried them out.

He quickly developed a great enthusiasm for chemistry. He used whatever money he could earn to buy chemicals from a local pharmacist.

Tom performed experiments in his room. His parents complained that he was making a mess and filling the house with bad odors. They made him move his experiments to the cellar. There he set up a small laboratory. To keep others from using his chemicals, he labeled all his bottles POISON.

Tom began spending much of his time in the

cellar. Sometimes accidents occurred. The sound of an explosion would occasionally echo through the house.

"He will blow us all up!" his father would exclaim.

His mother stayed calm. "Let him be," she would say. "He knows what he's about."

TRAIN BOY

AFTER THE EDISONS MOVED TO PORT Huron, life became more difficult. Sam Edison tried a variety of businesses. Not one was successful. The family was often close to poverty.

Mr. Edison operated a grocery store. He also tried the lumber business. He sold real estate. Sometimes the family earned money by taking in boarders, people who paid for their rooms and meals.

The Edison property included ten acres of rich farmland. Mr. Edison decided to raise vegetables on the land. Then he planned to sell the vegetables. Tom played an important role in the project. He later wrote:

After the field was ploughed [plowed], I . . . with a German boy about my age, did the planting. About eight acres were planted in sweet corn, the balance in radishes, onions, parsnips, and beets, etc.

I was very ambitious about this garden and worked very hard. My father had an old horse and wagon and with this we carried the vegetables to the town . . . and sold them from door to door.

One year I remember turning in to my mother six hundred dollars from the farm.

Tom soon became tired of farmwork, however. "Hoeing corn in the hot sun is not attractive," he wrote.

Then an opportunity to escape the farm presented itself. The railroad was coming to town. The Grand Trunk Railway had laid track between Port Huron and Detroit, about sixty miles to the south.

Tom heard there would be a job on the daily train for a boy to sell newspapers and snacks to passengers. Tom made up his mind to apply for the job.

In Port Huron, Michigan, the Edisons lived in this roomy wood-frame house. Tom's laboratory was in the basement.

Tom's mother didn't like the idea. She felt he was too young to be getting a job. His father felt differently. He stuck up for Tom. Tom's earnings could help support the entire family, his father realized.

At the age of thirteen, Tom went to work for the Grand Trunk Railway. There would be no more schooling. His childhood was over.

It was not easy. Tom had to be out of bed at

6 A.M. At the Port Huron station, he boarded a train that left at 7:15 A.M.

As the train pulled out of the station, Tom's workday began. Carrying a basket, he made his way through the passenger cars. "Newspapers, apples, sandwiches, peanuts," he would call out.

The train arrived in Detroit at 10:30 A.M. The return train to Port Huron did not leave Detroit until 4:30 in the afternoon.

That meant that Tom had six hours to spend in Detroit, a big, busy city of about 50,000 people. Tom found many places where he could buy the supplies and equipment that he needed for his experiments.

Then Tom got the idea of setting up a small laboratory on the train. The conductor gave him permission to use an empty space in the baggage car. Tom was then able to use his free time to conduct experiments.

Tom's baggage-car laboratory had a short life. One day a jar that held a dangerous chemical called phosphorus fell from the shelves. Exposed to air, the phosphorus burst into flames. The fire quickly

Edison at age fourteen. At the time, he worked selling newspapers and snacks to passengers on the Grand Trunk Railway.

spread. The baggage-master rushed to the scene to smother the flames.

This incident is another reason Tom lost some of his hearing. He recalled that the baggage-master "got a bad burn and boxed my ears so that I got somewhat deaf thereafter."

Edison later said his hearing loss was caused by another event. One day he had to race after the train as it was leaving the station. A conductor grabbed him by the ears and pulled him aboard. "I felt something pop inside my head," Edison later recalled, "and my deafness started from that time."

Some historians believe there were other reasons

for Tom's hearing loss. They say that scarlet fever and other childhood diseases may have caused it.

Whatever the reason, Edison began to realize that he was having difficulty hearing while working on the train. He later wrote, "I haven't heard a bird sing since I was twelve years old."

His hearing loss made Tom more shy and serious. He spent more time by himself. Books and experiments became even more important to him.

"My refuge became the Detroit Public Library," he later wrote. "I started...with the first book on the bottom shelf and went through the lot, one by one...I didn't read a few books. I read the library."

After the fire on the train, Tom was no longer allowed to store chemicals in the baggage car. But he was given permission to set up a small printing press there. He began to publish his own newspaper. It reported news and gossip that he gathered on the train. A weekly paper, it cost four cents.

Tom's lack of schooling was obvious in the stories that he wrote. He spelled words the way that they sounded. Sure became "shure." Opposition appeared

Port Huron, Michigan (above), where the Edison family settled in 1854, was linked to Detroit by the Grand Trunk Railway.

as "oppistion." The paper did not last very long. Tom's poor spelling and mistakes in grammar may have been reasons for its failure.

Tom had much greater success selling papers put out by others. These were troubled times in America. John Brown sought to start a slave rebellion in 1859. Abraham Lincoln was elected president in 1860. The next year, Fort Sumter was fired upon, and the Civil War began. Newspapers kept people of the time informed of all that was happening.

One day in early April 1862, Tom arrived at the offices of the *Detroit Free Press* to pick up the newspapers he planned to sell. He saw an anxious crowd milling around in the street outside the newspaper office. The people were seeking word about a major battle that was being fought at a place called Shiloh in Tennessee. It was to be one of the bloodiest battles of the Civil War.

Tom knew that his newspapers would carry a much more complete account of the battle. There would be a tremendous demand for papers as a result.

"Here was a chance for enormous sales," he said, "if only the people along the line could know what happened. Suddenly an idea occurred to me."

Tom hurried back to the train station. There he sought out a telegraph operator. The telegraph is an instrument used to send messages over wires by electricity.

Tom asked the operator to send messages to all the stops along the line announcing what was happening at Shiloh. He promised to give the operator free newspapers and magazines for doing him this favor.

That was part one of his plan. Once the word had been received at the stations, part two would take effect. The stationmaster at each station would write brief Shiloh announcements on the blackboards usually used to list train schedules.

Tom usually purchased 200 copies of the *Detroit Free Press*. On this day, however, he ordered 1,000 copies.

Tom was even more successful than he had hoped. At every stop, people had read the short telegraphed message and wanted to know more. They made a frenzied rush for his papers. He could scarcely handle the demand.

"When I got to the first station . . . the platform was crowded with men and women. After one look at the crowd, I raised the price to ten cents. I sold thirty-five papers.

"At Mount Clemens, where I usually sold six papers, the crowd was there, too. I raised the price to fifteen cents."

A huge crowd was also on hand when the train pulled into Port Huron. "I then yelled, 'Twenty-five cents, gentlemen! I haven't enough to go around!'"

Tom was thrilled with the huge amount of money he earned. And he was also impressed with the role that the telegraph had played. "It was then it struck me that the telegraph was just about the best thing going," Tom said. "I determined at once to become a telegrapher."

TRAMP TELEGRAPHER

TOM HAD ALWAYS BEEN INTERESTED in the telegraph. Working on the railroad had only expanded his interest in the device.

Samuel F. B. Morse had invented the telegraph in 1837, about ten years before Tom was born. Before the telegraph, messages sent over long distances were delivered by men on horseback. There was no faster way. To the people of the mid-1800s, the telegraph seemed almost magical in what it was able to do.

When he was fifteen, Edison built his own telegraph system. He strung wire to the home of Jim Clancy, a young friend, about a mile away.

```
a .-       n -.
b -...     o ---
c -.-.     p .--.
d -..      q --.-
e .        r .-.
f ..-.     s ...
g --.      t -
h ....     u ..-
i ..       v ...-
j .---     w .--
k -.-      x -..-
l .-..     y -.--
m --       z --..

1 .----    6 -....
2 ..---    7 --...
3 ...--    8 ---..
4 ....-    9 ----.
5 .....    0 -----
```

In the Morse code, short and long sounds (dots and dashes) are used to represent letters and numerals.

"It worked fine," Tom later recalled.

Tom and Jim Clancy often sent messages back and forth in Morse code. Morse code is a system of communicating based upon the sharp sounds, or clicks, that a telegraph produces. A click followed by a short interval is called a dot. A click followed by a long interval is called a dash.

Each letter of the alphabet has its own dot-and-dash combination. The letter "A" is a dot followed by a dash, the letter "B" is a dash followed by three dots, and so on.

The fact that he could not hear well was not a drawback to Tom. He could hear the telegraph's clicks quite clearly. What he did not hear was bothersome background noise.

When Tom returned home at night, he would

practice with Jim Clancy. It was always late when he arrived home, usually around 10 P.M. His father would try to get him to go to bed.

But Tom figured out a way to outwit his father. Mr. Edison liked to read the unsold newspapers that Tom brought home. So Tom stopped bringing any newspapers back. Instead, he told his father that the Clancys got the newspaper. He could get Jim Clancy to send him the day's important stories by telegraph.

Mr. Edison liked the idea. He allowed Tom to stay up until midnight or even later.

Tom went about the task of receiving Jim Clancy's messages. He listened intently as the telegraph clicked out the dots and dashes. In pencil, he wrote down the words that the letters formed.

But Tom was slow. A topflight telegrapher could receive forty or fifty words a minute. Tom didn't even approach that speed.

Tom knew that he needed to improve in order to get a job as a telegrapher. Fortunately, he found someone who was willing to help him improve his speed and skill.

James MacKenzie was the stationmaster at Mount Clemens, one of the stops between Port Huron and Detroit. He was an expert telegrapher. Tom had once saved MacKenzie's three-year-old son from a tragic accident. Tom had spotted the boy on the train tracks. A boxcar was rolling toward him. Tom threw aside the bundle of newspapers he was carrying, made a rush for the boy, and snatched him off the tracks.

MacKenzie was deeply grateful. When he heard that Tom wanted to learn to be a telegraph operator, he offered to teach him.

Tom also kept his job with the railroad. He still boarded the train each day. But he traveled only as far as Mount Clemens, where he would get off the train to work with MacKenzie.

There were many job opportunities for young telegraphers. The Civil War was raging. Hundreds of operators had gone into the military to fight. They had left their jobs. Those jobs were now available to Tom and other young men like him.

In the summer of 1863, Tom finished training with MacKenzie. He felt ready to go to work as a telegrapher. He was fifteen.

The Mount Clemens, Michigan, station on the Grand Trunk Railway, where Tom trained to be a telegrapher.

His first job was at the town telegraph office in Port Huron. The office was in one corner of a jewelry store. It was not a busy office. Messages (called telegrams) were few. Tom didn't mind. When not sending or receiving, he read back issues of *Scientific American*, which were available at the office. He also practiced to improve his speed as an operator.

In the spring of 1864, Tom moved on to a job as a railway telegrapher. Railroads used the telegraph to communicate between stations. By reporting the movement of trains, the device enabled the railroads to become more efficient. The telegraph also helped to cut down on accidents.

Tom became an operator at a small Canadian station on the Grand Trunk Railway in Stratford, Ontario. He worked the night shift, from 7 P.M. to 7 A.M. Since there were not many messages to be handled, Tom usually read or napped.

The Grand Trunk Railway had a rule that each operator had to send a signal to the main office every half hour. The signal showed that he was at his desk and not asleep.

This order annoyed Tom. But he soon found a way to outsmart it. He devised a clocklike mechanism that he linked to the telegraph's sending system. It didn't matter whether Tom happened to be reading or napping. Every half hour the device automatically sent the appropriate signal to the main office.

For the next several years, from 1864 to 1868, Tom was one of hundreds of young telegraphers who traveled from one place to another in search of better jobs and higher pay. They were known as "tramp" operators.

Tom hooked up a clever, clocklike device to his telegraph's sending system. The invention allowed Tom to nap, if he wished.

Tom sometimes held several jobs a year, all in different places. From Stratford, Ontario, he moved on to Adrian, Michigan. He turned up next in Fort Wayne, Indiana, and then Indianapolis, Indiana. In February 1865, he started work in Cincinnati, Ohio.

After the Civil War had ended, in the spring of 1866, he landed in Louisville, Kentucky. There he remained for more than a year.

There was no glamour to his life. He usually slept in shabby boarding houses. The telegraph offices were seedy and cluttered. The office in Cincinnati was infested with rats.

He turned the room he rented in Cincinnati into a combination lab and library. "I began to frequent secondhand bookstores and acquired quite a library," he said.

Tom wasn't always a devoted worker. Sometimes he would become occupied while reading a scientific book or article. At such times, he might let messages that he was supposed to be sending pile up for hours.

Other times, as Tom was receiving messages, an idea would come to him. He would quickly send a message to the other operator telling him to stop. Then he would grab a notebook and jot down his thoughts.

Tom was always trying to improve his speed as an operator. He even developed a new and unusual style of handwriting. He printed his letters and made each as small as possible. On a sheet of paper about the size of this page, he could crowd more than 600 words. Each was clear and easy to read. This style enabled him to become much faster in making written copies of telegraph messages.

Edison eventually did realize his ambition of becoming a first-class operator. As such, he was paid around $125 a month. That was a very good salary for the time.

As soon as he received his pay, however, Edison would buy parts and equipment for his experiments. As a result, even though he made a good living, he was almost always short of money.

In the fall of 1867,

Tom in his late teens. At the time, he worked as a professional telegrapher, often changing jobs as he moved about the country.

the twenty-year-old Edison returned to Port Huron to visit his parents. He did not stay long. "After stopping for some time at home, I got restless," Edison said, "and thought I would like to work in the East."

While at his parents' home, Edison was in touch with Milt Adams, a friend in Boston, Massachusetts. Edison asked Adams whether there might be an operator's job there. Adams said there was an opening at Western Union, the nation's largest telegraph company.

At the time, Boston was the center of scientific learning. Many inventors whom Edison had heard of lived there.

By this time, Edison had come to realize that he wasn't crazy about being a telegraph operator. The technical side of telegraphy was what interested him. At each location where he had worked, he had improved the telegraph equipment. He wanted to spend more time studying and inventing. In Boston, he felt he would be able to do that.

FIRST
INVENTIONS

EDISON ARRIVED IN BOSTON EARLY in 1868. He looked like a country boy. He wore a wide-brimmed hat and baggy clothes.

When he walked into the office of Western Union to apply for a job, he felt ill at ease. "I had been four days and nights on the road," he recalled, "and having had very little sleep, did not present a very fresh or stylish appearance . . ."

The way he looked didn't bother the people at Western Union. When they learned how skilled Edison was as an operator, they hired him right away.

Edison was assigned to work nights. He liked

that. During the day, he could explore Boston. He could also work on his experiments.

Edison's mind was filled with ideas. "I am now twenty-one. I may live to be fifty," Edison said to his friend Milt Adams. "I have got so much to do and life is so short, I'm going to hustle."

At the time, Edison was working on a new model of the telegraph. It could send two messages at once over the same wire. It was called a duplex. Tom produced a working model of the duplex after only two months in Boston.

To telegraph companies, the duplex was of great value. Using it, a company could double the number of messages it sent over the same number of wires.

Two other inventors had also created duplexes. But Edison's duplex was written about in *The Telegrapher*. The journal described it as "simple and ingenious."

This article caught the attention of investors. They offered to provide the money to support Edison's experiments. In return, they would receive part of any profits the inventions might produce.

The duplex was only one of Edison's interests at the time. He was also working on an electric vote recorder.

He hoped that the recorder would be used by the Massachusetts state legislature when they voted on new laws. Under the system then in use, a roll call vote was taken. The name of the lawmaker would be announced. He would then vote by saying "aye" (yes) or "no."

To Edison, this seemed like a terrible waste of time. His invention made voting much simpler. He described how it worked:

> In front of each member of the House [would be] two buttons, one for aye and one for no. When the vote was called for, each member pressed one or another of the buttons before him. The number of votes appeared automatically on the record.

For the invention, Edison received his first patent. This is a right granted by the government to a person by which he or she is the only one allowed to make or sell the invention. Edison would be granted more than 1,000 patents during his lifetime.

Edison expected the automatic vote recorder to earn money for him. But lawmakers turned their back on the invention. They preferred the old system. With roll-call voting, each legislator had the chance to speak at length about a bill. By doing so, the bill's passage could be delayed. Slowing the voting worked to the advantage of some lawmakers. Edison's automatic system would put an end to the delaying tactics. It worked too well.

Edison later said that he was "crushed" by what had happened. "The electric vote recorder got no further than the Patent Office," he noted.

But Tom had learned an important lesson. In the future, he would invent only products for which there was a demand.

Edison continued to be interested in the telegraph and devices related to it. One of these was the stock ticker. The stock ticker sent out minute-by-minute price information about stocks or gold. It got its name from the ticking sound its printer made.

Edison received his first patent for this electric vote recorder. The lack of demand for the instrument was a disappointment to him.

Edison developed a number of improvements for the stock ticker. His own model of the device earned him his second patent. He sold his rights to the device to a large telegraph company.

Edison's success enabled him to leave his job at Western Union. A notice in *The Telegrapher* told of his move. Edison would now "devote his time to

Early in his career, Edison became deeply involved with the stock ticker, which sent out minute-by-minute price information about stocks and gold to traders.

bringing out his inventions," said the magazine. He had realized one of his chief goals in life.

Edison continued working to improve his duplex telegraph. A large telegraph company was interested in the device. But when Edison tested his duplex over the wires between Rochester, New York, and New York City, the instrument failed.

The failure was a serious setback for Edison. It put him heavily in debt. He felt he had no future in

Boston. In the spring of 1869, Edison borrowed a few dollars from a friend and set off for New York City.

When he arrived, he did not have a cent in his pockets. He called on Frank Pope, a telegraph expert. Pope was an official of the Gold Indicator Company. The firm was a leader in providing minute-to-minute changes in the price of gold. Pope had heard of Edison's work in Boston.

Edison admitted that he had no place to sleep. Pope provided him with a cot in the cellar of a company building.

While Edison was waiting for a job to open, Pope asked him to study his company's telegraph equipment. One day, Edison happened to be in the company's offices when the equipment sending out gold prices broke down. Pope and other workers could not discover what was wrong. All over New York, tickers fell silent.

Dr. Samuel Laws, who owned the company, burst out of his office. He was in a state of panic. He began to yell at everyone. Edison later described Laws as "the most excited person I have ever seen."

Edison looked the equipment over carefully. He found the problem.

"Fix it! Fix it!" Laws yelled. "Quick, for God's sake!"

Edison made the repairs. The next day, Dr. Laws offered Edison a job that paid well. Edison accepted the offer.

Edison did not work for Dr. Laws very long. He and Pope formed their own company to report gold and stock prices.

Pope handled the company's business matters. Edison made the equipment that the company needed. For his workshop, Edison rented space in Jersey City, New Jersey. The city was a quick ferry ride across the Hudson River from New York.

Edison was soon involved in many other ventures. He pushed himself hard. Sometimes he worked sixteen-hour days. He opened a second workshop in Newark, New Jersey. Dozens of people worked for him there.

Within a year, Edison developed a device that vastly improved stock tickers. He sold the invention for $40,000. That was a small fortune for a man as young as Edison.

About a year after the Newark shop began operation, Edison's mother died. He traveled back to Michigan for the funeral. But he did not stay long. He quickly returned to New Jersey and his many projects.

At twenty-three, Edison had already made great strides as an inventor. He was looked upon as one of the nation's foremost experts at sending information over wires. He was respected as an inventor. His passion for inventing would soon earn him great acclaim.

INVENTION FACTORY

EDISON LIKED TO SLEEP LATE. AFTER breakfast, he would read several newspapers. He would also read whatever scientific journals that came in the mail.

By mid-afternoon, he was at his Newark workshop. He usually began working in the early evening. Around midnight, he had a meal. It was often just a piece of pie or cake and a glass of milk. After eating, he would continue working for several more hours.

Tom liked to tell people that he did not need sleep. But he took long naps at his workshop. He would stretch out, fully clothed, on a bench or worktable. Sometimes he would sleep on the

Edison kept his Newark workshop and laboratory in operation for six years. It was the first of his "invention factories."

floor. "He would go to sleep anywhere, any time, on anything," said Alfred Tate, one of his assistants.

Edison was not an easy person to work for. He wanted his employees to work as hard as he worked. That meant working long into the night. It meant working weekends as well as weekdays.

Toward the end of 1871, Edison's life changed abruptly. He met and fell in love with a pretty sixteen-year-old woman named Mary Stillwell.

He was introduced to her by one of his employees. Soon after they met, Edison offered to get her employment at his shop in Newark. She took a job punching small holes in paper telegraph tape.

Edison courted her in an unusual way. He would visit the shop and stand and admire her.

Having Edison stare at her made the young woman nervous. One day, she dropped her hands into her lap and said, "Oh, Mr. Edison, I can always tell when you are near me."

Edison finally got up enough courage to speak to her about his feelings. "Miss Stillwell," he said, "I've been thinking of you considerably. If you are willing to have me, I'd like to marry you."

The young woman was stunned. She told Edison that he frightened her.

"Think it over," Edison continued. "Talk to your mother and let me know what she says."

Edison's success and money made him an attractive prospect as a husband. The next day, Mary told Edison that her mother approved of the match.

Edison began calling on Mary at home. They

often sat together in the parlor with her parents present.

Edison taught Mary the Morse code. That made it possible for him to "speak" privately to Mary by tapping dots and dashes into her palm.

The couple married on Christmas Day, 1871. They moved into a new house in Newark.

Tom and Mary were to have three children. The first, a daughter named Marion, was born in 1873. Edison nicknamed her Dot.

The Edisons's second child, a son named Thomas, Jr., was born in 1876. Edison gave him the nickname Dash.

Their third child, a second son, was born in 1878. He was named William.

Edison adored his children, but he seldom saw them. He was wrapped up in his work. He kept much the same schedule as he had before his marriage. He would work a good part of the day and most of the night. Arriving home in the early morning, he fell into his bed exhausted.

The many hours that her husband spent at the lab

Mary Stillwell, whom Edison married in 1871. The couple had three children together.

saddened his wife. She felt neglected, but Tom scarcely noticed.

At the time, Edison was working on an improved version of the telegraph. It was called the quadruplex.

Telegraphy was now vital to the business life of the nation. As a result, telegraph wires were now crowded with messages. The quadruplex could send four messages at a time over the same wires.

During the early months of 1873, Edison worked without letup on improvements to the duplex. This would help him create the quadruplex. After several weeks of work, he jotted down the results in a laboratory workbook. "I experimented 22 nights, tried 22 duplex systems, 9 failures, 4 partial successes. 10 all right, 1 or 2 bad."

Edison was finally successful. He staged a demonstration of the quadruplex on July 9, 1874. It was a success. The invention was called "one of the most important contributions to the telegraph art."

Tom had agreed to sell the quadruplex to Western Union. But he and the company quarreled over money. Edison signed a contract to sell the device to a rival company. Lawsuits and trials followed.

Despite the legal problems, Edison continued to work as hard as ever. Several new inventions came from his active mind. One was an electric pen.

The pen was powered by a tiny electric motor connected to a battery. Its chief feature was its pointed tip, which moved up and down rapidly.

The pen's tip was used to make a series of tiny holes

The advertisement for Edison's Electric Pen and Press announced "many thousands now in use."

in a sheet of waxed paper. The paper then became a stencil. Ink or paint could be pressed through the paper to reproduce the letters or designs.

When Tom opened his workshop in Newark, he said he hoped to make it an "invention factory." It became just that. It remained in operation for six years. In that time, Edison was granted about 200 patents for work done there.

By the mid-1870s, Tom realized that he had outgrown the factory in Newark. He also needed more room for Mary and their growing family. It was time for a change.

MENLO PARK

L ATE IN DECEMBER 1875, EDISON bought a house and land in Menlo Park, New Jersey. Menlo Park was a small farming community about twelve miles south of Newark.

Edison had a long, two-story wood-frame structure built on the property. It looked like a dormitory or barracks. The building was his laboratory.

Tom set a goal for himself at Menlo Park. He said he wanted to bring out a "minor invention every ten days and a big thing every six months or so."

Edison also bought a farmhouse in Menlo Park for his family. The house was only a few hundred

The Edison research complex at Menlo Park, New Jersey, in the winter of 1880 to 1881. The long, narrow building is the main laboratory.

yards from Tom's lab. But Mary Edison rarely saw her husband. He was still absorbed in his work.

At the time, Edison was continuing his experiments with the telegraph. But the instrument's popularity was beginning to fade. On March 7, 1876, Alexander Graham Bell, a teacher of deaf people in Boston, was granted a patent for the telephone. The telephone was beginning to replace the telegraph in the nation's offices and factories.

But Bell's telephone did not work well. It was not very loud. A person had to shout into it to be heard on the other end of the line. Even then, the listener heard only a whisper. And the whisper was all but blotted out by static.

The problem with Bell's telephone was a device called the transmitter. A thin disk of iron, the transmitter converted sound waves into electrical waves.

Edison was fascinated by the telephone. He worked to improve the instrument. Charles Batchelor, a skilled draftsman, helped him. Batchelor took Edison's ideas and made detailed drawings based on them.

With Batchelor's help, Edison devised a disk-shaped transmitter made of rubber and carbon. It looked like a small button. With a carbon-button transmitter, a person's voice was clear and distinct when heard on the telephone.

Through his research with the telephone, Edison learned more about the quality of sound. Sound waves, he knew, produced their own shapes. Could

Alexander Graham Bell invented the telephone, but Edison's version of the instrument (above) produced sound that was louder and clearer.

these shapes be recorded in some way? If so, it might then be possible to replay them.

These thoughts caused Edison to start work on a new invention. It was the phonograph, or record player.

To try to record sound, Edison began to experiment with diaphragms. The type of diaphragm he used was a thin disk, usually made of paper or metal. It vibrated when sound was directed at it.

One day, Edison attached a small, blunt pin to the center of a diaphragm. Then he placed a strip of waxed paper beneath the point of the pin.

"I rigged up an instrument hastily and pulled a strip of paper through it," he said, "at the same time shouting, 'Halloo!'" The vibrations from Edison's voice made marks on the waxed paper.

Then Edison took the paper and pulled it through again. This time the marks on the waxed paper vibrated a pin attached to a second diaphragm.

"My friend Batchelor and I listened breathlessly," said Edison. "We heard a distinct sound, which a strong imagination might have translated into the original 'Halloo.'"

More experiments followed. Late in 1877, Edison had sketches for a talking machine. On December 4, 1877, the machine was ready for testing. It consisted

The main laboratory's upper floor. Shelves holding chemicals line the walls.

of a rotating cylinder on which sounds were to be recorded. Two diaphragms, each fitted with a needle, were mounted at the opposite ends of the cylinder.

As the workers looked on, Edison wrapped a sheet of tinfoil around the cylinder. Then he turned a handle that caused the cylinder to rotate. At the same time he spoke these words into one of the diaphragms:

> *Mary had a little lamb,*
> *Its fleece was white as snow,*
> *And everywhere that Mary went*
> *The lamb was sure to go.*

Then Tom took the needle of the second diaphragm. He placed it into the groove that had been traced in the tinfoil by his voice's vibrations. He turned the crank again. As the cylinder rotated, Edison's voice could be heard repeating the little nursery rhyme.

The onlookers gasped in amazement. Edison

Edison posed with his phonograph for this well-known photograph in 1878 when he visited Washington, D.C.

himself was in awe of what he had created. "Everybody was astonished," he said.

In April 1878, Edison demonstrated his invention to members of Congress in Washington, D.C. He took it to the White House to show to President Rutherford B. Hayes.

Of all his inventions, Edison liked the phonograph the most. "This is my favorite," he once said, "and I expect it to grow up and be a big feller [fellow]..."

The phonograph did indeed become a "big feller." It earned Edison the nickname the Wizard of Menlo Park and brought him worldwide fame. It gave rise to the huge music recording industry. It grew beyond anything Edison might have dreamed.

A BETTER
CANDLE

DURING THE SPRING OF 1878, EDISON felt tired and ill. That summer he took a long vacation. He joined other scientists on a tour of the Rocky Mountains. He also visited the California coast.

When he returned to Menlo Park, Tom was rested and refreshed. A new field attracted him. He began experimenting with electric lighting.

In the 1870s, homes outside of big cities were lit with candles and oil lamps. There was always a danger of fire.

In city homes, apartments, and offices, lamps that burned gas were often used. But gaslights were smelly. They were also a fire hazard.

Many inventors sought to overcome these problems with electric lighting. Much of their work focused on the filament. This is the threadlike structure within a lightbulb. When electricity flows into the filament, it glows and gives off light.

But no one had been able to find the right filament material. The filaments that had been tried burned for only a few moments.

Edison decided to take up the challenge. "I have let the other inventors get the start of me in this matter," said Edison. "But I believe I can catch up with them now."

Edison and his men tried filaments of many different substances. They tried copper and steel, boron and gold, and nickel and chromium. They made test filaments of different lengths and thicknesses. They doubled them over. They formed them into hairpin shapes. They fashioned them into spirals and double spirals.

For each test, the air had to be pumped out of a glass bulb before the filament could be tested. This created a vacuum within the bulb.

Oxygen in the air makes things burn quickly. But

when the test material was burned within a vacuum, it burned longer. It also burned brighter.

Months went by. Edison and his workers would carefully place each test filament in a pear-shaped glass bulb. The air would be pumped out, and the current would be turned on. They would watch as the filament burned

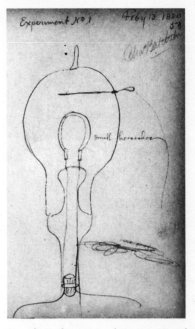

In this drawing from one of Edison's notebooks, the filament material had a horseshoe shape.

brightly for a moment or two. Then it would smolder and die.

Edison remained confident, however. "The electric light has caused me the greatest amount of study and has required the most elaborate experiments," Edison later wrote. "I was never myself discouraged, or inclined to be hopeless of success."

Sometimes the work could be hazardous. One night, Edison and his men were testing a wire made of nickel. The material burned so brightly that it hurt their eyes.

Edison's notebook for January 27, 1879, reads: "Owing to the enormous power of the light, my eyes commenced to pain after seven hours' work, and I had to quit."

The next day he wrote, "Suffered [great pain] with my eyes last night. . . ."

But later the same day, he was able to write, "Eyes getting better."

Early in 1879, Edison began to experience the first hint of success with electric lighting. A very thin spiral of platinum was being tested at the time. It burned for "an hour or two," he noted.

That was good. But Edison knew that he could do better.

In the summer of 1879, Edison turned to carbon as a filament. Carbon was much cheaper than platinum. Tom and other inventors had tried carbon before, but it burned out too quickly.

By this time, however, Edison had created a better vacuum inside his test bulbs. He decided to test carbon under these new conditions.

Carbon was easy to obtain. Black soot was almost pure carbon. Soot was found on the inside of oil-lamp chimneys. Workers collected soot and mixed it with tar. They then rolled it into threadlike filaments. In some tests, the threads burned for an hour or two before burning out.

Edison believed he was on the right track. He and his assistants began testing different types of carbon filaments. Toward the end of October 1879, they turned to cotton thread.

They baked a length of thread in the oven, turning it to carbon. The carbonized thread was then formed into a horseshoe shape.

On the night of October 21, the thread was tested. "Before nightfall," Edison wrote, "the carbon was completed and inserted in the lamp. The bulb was exhausted of air and sealed, the current turned on, and the sight we had so long desired to see met our eyes."

In his Menlo Park laboratory, Edison works at baking filament material in a small furnace.

The bulb glowed dimly at first. Then, as the power of the electric current increased, it burned brighter and brighter.

Tom and his workers stared at the bulb in awe as it glowed on and on. An hour passed. Two hours.

Edison and his men continued to stare at the bulb. No one even thought of sleep. Other workers heard about what was happening. They filed into the room to gaze intently at the glowing bulb.

The bulb burned for more than half a day. It burned from 1:30 A.M. until almost 3:00 P.M.—about thirteen and a half hours.

When the glow finally faded, the men stood and cheered. But Edison was calm. He said, "If it can burn that number of hours, I know I can make it burn a hundred."

More testing followed. Cotton thread was a vegetable fiber. So Edison tested many other vegetable substances. He tried paper, cardboard, flax, wood shavings, fishing line, and coconut shell.

A thin strip of cardboard seemed to work the best. The cardboard was cut into a horseshoe shape. It was boiled in sugar and alcohol, then baked.

Once converted into carbon, the cardboard filament burned for 170 hours. On November 1, 1879, Edison applied for a patent for a carbon-filament lightbulb. It was quickly granted.

Soon after Edison's success, rumors began to

Edison's first successful electric lightbulb, with its hairpin-shaped carbon filament.

spread about his achievement. His Menlo Park neighbors told of brilliant lights in laboratory windows that burned all night long.

On Sunday, December 21, 1879, *The New York Herald* broke the story. The paper's headlines read:

EDISON'S LIGHT
THE GREAT INVENTOR'S TRIUMPH
IN ELECTRICAL ILLUMINATION

———————————

SUCCESS IN A COTTON THREAD

———————————

IT MAKES A LIGHT WITHOUT GAS
OR FLAME, CHEAPER THAN OIL

After the story appeared, many hundreds of curious visitors made their way to Menlo Park. Edison announced there would be an exhibition of electric lighting on New Year's Eve.

On the last day of December 1879, more than 3,000 people flooded into Menlo

Edison in 1878 at the age of thirty-one. His success with the electric light came the following year.

Park. Tom had strung electric lights from one tree to another leading to the laboratory. All of the laboratory rooms were lighted with Edison's lamps. Visitors were fascinated by being able to turn the lights on and off.

The *New York Tribune* declared it to be an example of "progress on the march." No one doubted the statement to be true.

Edison and his workers experimented with electric lighting for more than two years. There had been many dismal moments. But Edison had never thought of giving up.

"The trouble with other inventors is that they try a few things and they quit," Edison had told his workers. "I never quit until I get what I want." That kind of thinking brought him success.

A LIGHTING
SYSTEM

THE ELECTRIC LIGHTBULB WAS Edison's greatest invention. It is often called his "bright idea."

But the electric light was only part of the challenge that Edison faced. At the same time, he was working on a system that would deliver electricity into homes, offices, and factories. The system would carry an electric current to more than 1,000 electric lights. It would turn night into day.

Edison picked New York City for the location of the system. With so many people, New York had a high demand for electric lighting.

Early in 1881, Edison rented a four-story

mansion at 65 Fifth Avenue. It became his headquarters for the project.

"We're up in the world now!" thirty-four-year-old Edison told the *New York Tribune*.

> *I remember ten years ago. I had just come from Boston. I had to walk the streets of New York all night because I hadn't the price of a bed. And now think of it! I'm to occupy a whole house on Fifth Avenue.*

Edison realized that he could not light all of New York at one time. The city was too big. He picked out a site in lower Manhattan, east of City Hall. It covered about ten blocks. He chose a building at 257 Pearl Street for his power plant.

To generate power, Edison needed a dynamo. A dynamo is a machine that produces electrical energy. But Edison needed a dynamo bigger and more powerful than any ever built.

Tom assigned workers at Menlo Park to build such a dynamo. It was huge. It weighed about thirty

The "dynamo room" at Edison's Pearl Street generating plant.

tons. It was nicknamed "Jumbo" after a famous circus elephant.

Two Jumbos were eventually installed at the Pearl Street power plant. Edison connected the two and tried operating them together. A near-disaster occurred. "It was a terrifying experience," Edison recalled. "The engines and dynamos made a horrible racket, and the place seemed to be filled with sparks and flames of all colors."

Edison kept cool. He grabbed the control lever of one engine. A worker seized the lever controlling the other. Together they quickly shut down the machines. Edison eventually got the dynamos to operate properly. But the test rattled him.

To distribute power and light from the dynamos, Edison had to create all the parts required. None existed before this time.

Lightbulbs by the thousands were needed. Edison built a factory in Menlo Park to mass-produce bulbs. Within a year, more than 100 workers were employed there. Sockets also had to be made to hold the bulbs.

The wire necessary to connect the customers with the power plant presented a problem, too. The wire was too heavy to be strung on poles.

Edison decided to bury the wires beneath city streets. But in test burials, the wires leaked electricity. The ground became electrified as a result. To prevent leakage, Tom and his workers covered the wires with tar and other materials.

Switches were also needed so customers could

By 1881, Edison's lamp factory in Menlo Park was in operation. It employed more than 100 workers.

turn their lights on and off. Meters were needed to measure the amount of electricity customers used.

On September 4, 1882, the lighting system was ready to be tested. It was an important moment for Edison. "Success meant worldwide adoption of our central-station plan," Edison said. "Failure meant loss of money and prestige and the setting back of our enterprise."

In the final stages, Edison and his men worked

around the clock to complete the system. A celebration was planned. Edison went home to dress properly for the ceremonies. He put on a frock coat, striped trousers, and a top hat.

When Edison gave the signal, the switch was pulled. Instantly hundreds of lights burst into brightness. But there was no cheering. Edison, fearful that something might go wrong, had done little to promote the event. Only a few people were there for the historic moment.

"I was a little nervous," he admitted.

Despite the lack of fanfare, the little Pearl Street power plant was a beginning. It marked the dawning of the electric age. Before the twentieth century was very old, similar systems would light and power the entire world.

CHAPTER 10

A SECOND
MARRIAGE

INVENTING THE ELECTRIC LIGHTBULB and a system to deliver electric power took four years of Edison's life. At the time the Pearl Street plant in New York City went into operation, he was thirty-five.

Edison was becoming gray-haired now. But he still had a trim build and a youthful appearance.

His focus was changing. He no longer was merely an inventor. As he sought to build power stations in other cities of the Northeast, he was becoming one of the nation's most noted industrial leaders. He was also on his way to becoming a very wealthy man.

In the winter of 1881, Edison moved his family

to New York City. They lived in an apartment overlooking Gramercy Park. The family used their Menlo Park house as a summer home.

In the midst of his success, Edison was struck with tragedy. His wife Mary became seriously ill with typhoid fever during the summer of 1884. Eating spoiled food or drinking polluted water can cause typhoid fever.

At first, Mary's illness did not alarm the family. But when she did not get better, Mary's sister, Alice, moved into the Menlo Park home to care for her.

Mary's condition grew worse. Edison hurried back from New York. He was with her when she died on August 9, 1884.

His wife's death was a heavy blow. Edison's daughter later wrote that her father was "shaking with grief, weeping and sobbing." Edison seldom went back to Menlo Park after Mary's death. The famous laboratory fell into decay.

At thirty-seven, Edison was a single father with three young children to raise. His two sons, Tom, who was eight, and William, six years old, went to live with their Aunt Alice in Menlo Park. His daughter, Marion, attended boarding school in New York City. She was thirteen, tall, and blond.

Edison delighted in Marion's company. He took her to the theater and fine restaurants. On Sundays, they went on carriage drives together.

Marion sometimes planned meals that her father liked. She learned to play his favorite songs on the piano.

At the time, Edison was deeply involved in the electrical industry. The Pearl Street power plant was a springboard. It led Edison to begin building power plants in other cities.

He also began manufacturing electrical parts and equipment. "If there are no factories to make my inventions," he said, "I will build the factories myself."

Edison set up a factory in Menlo Park to make lightbulbs. By 1881, the factory employed more than 100 workers. The company eventually produced more than a million lightbulbs a year.

Another of his factories made motors and

dynamos. Called the Edison Machine Works, it was located in New York City.

Edison later moved the Edison Machine Works to Schenectady, New York, in 1886 because of labor troubles. It became a huge operation. It occupied a factory that stretched "for miles." About 18,000 workers were employed there.

Early in 1885, Tom traveled to Boston to visit friends. While there, he met a young woman named Mina Miller. She was the daughter of a wealthy manufacturer from Akron, Ohio. Mina was eighteen, almost twenty years younger than Edison was. She attended a private school in Boston.

Mina was poised and confident. Edison was now one of the most famous men of the day. He was a millionaire. Even so, Mina was not in awe of him.

On the other hand, Mina dazzled Tom. When they were together, he could not take his eyes off of her. She was always in his thoughts. "Got thinking of Mina," Edison wrote upon returning to New York, "and came near being run over by a street car."

Tom made up his mind to marry Mina. He visited her often. He wrote and telegraphed her.

The Edisons' Glenmont home in West Orange, New Jersey, had twenty-six rooms, plus a greenhouse, stable, and other buildings.

He taught Mina how to send and receive Morse code. Late in the summer of 1885, he tapped an important question into Mina's hand. "I asked her in Morse code if she would marry me," Edison later wrote. "The word 'yes' is an easy one to send in telegraphic signals, and she sent it." The two were married on February 24, 1886.

Neither Tom nor his bride were very fond of city living. After their marriage, they settled in West Orange, New Jersey, just north and west of Newark.

Mina Miller Edison with daughter, Madeleine, the first of her three children.

Edison bought a hilltop mansion there. It was named Glenmont. It had twenty-six rooms. The thirteen-acre site included a barn, greenhouse, and stable.

Edison had never lived in such luxury before. "When I entered this, I was paralyzed," he said. "It was a great deal too nice for me."

Mina, however, felt at ease there. She called herself Glenmont's "home executive." She hired and fired the servants. She paid the bills.

Tom and Mina had three children. They were born in an upstairs bedroom at Glenmont. Madeleine was born in 1888. She was followed by Charles in 1890, and Theodore in 1898.

Edison's other children, Marion, Tom, and William, began a new life, too. They moved to Glenmont to live with their father and stepmother.

Mina quickly came to realize her husband's top priority was his work. "He invents all the time," she noted, "even in his sleep."

CHAPTER 11

WEST ORANGE

NOT LONG AFTER HIS MARRIAGE TO Mina, Edison bought fourteen acres of land in West Orange, New Jersey. The site was less than a mile from Glenmont, the Edison home. There, Edison built a huge research complex.

The West Orange operation was at least ten times bigger than Menlo Park. The main lab was 250 feet long and three stories high. Four smaller labs were nearby. All were equipped with the latest machinery and finest instruments.

As many as 200 people worked at the West Orange lab. They included many scientists and engineers. Hundreds of Edison's patents were developed there.

Edison's research complex in West Orange, New Jersey, included a three-story main laboratory and several smaller labs.

Edison promised that West Orange would bring into being "useful things that every man, woman, and child wants...at a price they could afford to pay."

Most of the work at West Orange concerned electrical research. New types of lamps, meters, and generators to produce electricity were always being developed and tested.

Edison also became interested in the phonograph

again. More than ten years had passed since Edison had first recorded sound. Other inventors had been working to improve the phonograph. One was Alexander Graham Bell.

Edison had recorded sound on tinfoil. Bell's phonograph replaced the tinfoil with a cylinder made of wax-coated cardboard. Better sound often resulted. In addition, wax-coated cylinders were more durable. Edison's tinfoil cylinders were easily damaged.

Edison was furious. He didn't like anyone tinkering with what was his favorite invention. He felt as if he were being robbed. He called Bell and his associates a "bunch [of] pirates."

Edison vowed to create a better phonograph than Bell's. He began work on an improved machine in 1886.

Tom did not let the fact that he had poor hearing stop him. To test the phonograph, he would put his ear in contact with the cone-shaped speaker from which the sound came.

Other times he would bite down on the sound speaker. The vibrations would travel through the bones in his head to his ears. "It takes a deaf man to hear," Edison would say.

Tom kept track of his progress in his notebooks. He jotted down a long list of problems that he found. These included "crackling sounds," "knocking sound," "chips in wax cylinder," and "humming sound due to motor." One by one, Edison solved these and other problems.

Edison's new phonograph had great appeal. The sound was recorded on a solid wax cylinder. It was easy to replace one cylinder with another.

Tom recorded popular singers of the day. The most noted musicians also made recordings on his wax cylinders.

Business boomed. Recordings sold by the millions.

Its ease of operation helped to make the phonograph popular. "Even a child can operate it," Edison said.

To make phonographs, Tom built a huge factory

Edison in 1906 with a cylinder phonograph. Edison did not begin producing disk records until 1909.

next to his West Orange lab. Hundreds of workers were employed there. He built a second factory to make fancy wooden cabinets for the phonographs.

Rival companies competed with Edison. During the 1890s, some of these companies made phonographs that played flat disk records. The public liked disks better than cylinders. Disks were easier to store, and had longer playing times.

Edison was slow to switch to disk recordings. Not until 1909 did he begin producing disks.

Phonographs and disk records stayed popular until the mid-1980s. They then began to be replaced by cassette tapes and compact discs. Compact discs are much smaller and last longer than phonograph records. The sound that compact disc players produce is better than the sound from record players.

Millions of record players are still in use, however. Older records are played on them. But most people use cassette players or compact disc players for listening to recorded music. They are the most recent examples of success in recording the human voice.

Within his labs in West Orange, Edison pursued many other interests besides the phonograph. One of these was the mining of metals. Late in 1888, he began devoting more and more time to this subject.

Edison created a simple method of separating

particles of iron from the rock in which they were found. Edison's idea was based on the use of powerful magnets.

After the metal-bearing rock, or ore, was taken from the mine, it was crushed until it became like fine sand. It was then poured down a chute past a magnet, which attracted the tiny iron particles. The waste sand continued down the chute.

Edison built a huge plant at Ogdensburg, New Jersey, to process iron ore. Giant steam shovels removed the iron ore from the earth. Powerful rock crushers reduced the ore to powder.

The mining operation was one of Edison's few failures. The equipment often broke down. Steelmakers rejected Edison's ore. They said it was not pure enough.

Edison spent more than two million dollars of his own money on the mining venture. Other investors poured in a million dollars more.

Tom shrugged off the losses. "Well, it's gone," he said of the money. "But we had a ... good time spending it."

Edison at his ore-processing operation at Ogdensburg, New Jersey.

The mining operation was not a total loss. It led Edison to become interested in limestone. From clay and crushed limestone, cement is made.

Edison set up a company to make cement from limestone. The operation produced 1,000 barrels of cement a day.

A highway built of Edison cement is still in use in New Jersey. Yankee Stadium in New York City is also made of cement provided by Edison's company.

MAKING MOVIES

NOT LONG AFTER EDISON'S RESEARCH site opened in West Orange, New Jersey, the inventor had an important visitor. His name was Eadweard Muybridge.

Muybridge was a British photographer. He was famous for his photographs of people and animals in motion. Each series of photos was made up of a dozen or so connected images. Athletes were shown running or jumping. Horses galloped. Birds streaked through the sky.

Tom was fascinated by Muybridge's work. At the time, improving the phonograph was Edison's chief interest. Yet the idea of a camera that could record motion excited him. More and more, it began to occupy his mind.

Edison spoke about his idea to one of his assistants, a young Englishman named W. K. L. Dickson. Dickson was skilled in the art of photography. He often experimented with cameras and film.

Together, Edison and Dickson began developing a motion picture camera. On October 8, 1888, Edison applied for his first camera patent. The document said, "I am experimenting upon an instrument which does for the eye what the phonograph does for the ear."

One problem involved feeding the film through the camera at a controlled speed. To help solve the problem, Edison sent Dickson to Rochester, New York, to meet with George Eastman. Eastman was an inventor in the field of photography. He was about to introduce the Kodak camera.

Eastman used film made of a light, flexible plastic, called celluloid. Edison asked Eastman to make a strip of celluloid film that was fifty feet long. When Tom saw the long film strip for the first time, he broke into a wide smile. "That's it!" he said. "We've got it!"

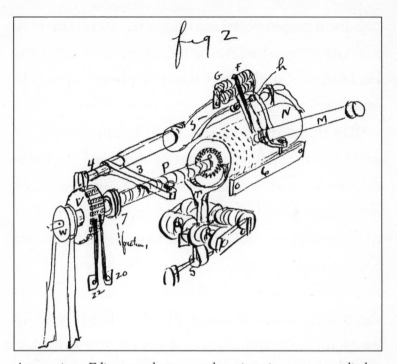

At one time, Edison sought to record motion pictures on a cylinder-shaped device, as he had recorded sound. This Edison sketch dates to October 1888.

Later in 1889, Edison and Dickson had completed work on their motion picture camera. They called it a kinetograph.

To view his moving pictures, Edison created what he called a Kinetoscope. The apparatus was housed in a tall wooden cabinet that had a peephole at the top. As a battery-powered motor advanced the film, the viewer watched the moving images through the peephole. Each "movie" lasted only about ninety seconds.

Edison fitted the cabinet with a coin slot. It cost a nickel to view the moving film inside. Coin-operated Kinetoscopes were called "peep shows." They were a big hit in entertainment arcades.

Edison's next challenge was to make an "enlarged Kinetoscope." It would project the moving image onto a large screen in a theater.

Other inventors were also working on film projectors. Thomas Armat, a young inventor from Washington, D.C., was one of the first to develop such a machine. He named it the Vitascope.

Soon, Armat and Edison joined forces. The Vitascope was manufactured and sold under Edison's name.

On the night of April 23, 1896, the Vitascope was introduced at a music hall in New York City. The realism of the films was a new experience for people. They oohed and aahed. A filmed sequence of waves

Introduced in 1896 and marketed under Edison's name, the Vitascope projected motion picture images onto a large theater screen.

crashing on a beach frightened viewers in the front row. They jumped back in panic.

Newspapers of the day hailed the Vitascope. They called it "Edison's latest triumph." The praise made Tom uncomfortable. He knew that it was Armat who deserved the credit.

Edison also made his own movies. At West Orange, he built the world's first motion picture

One of Edison's earliest movies pictured a man's sneeze from beginning to end.

studio. Its roof and sides were covered with black roofing paper. It looked like a small barn.

Sections of the studio's slanted roof could be swung open to let in the sunlight, which was needed for filming.

The studio rested on a circular track. When filming, the studio could be rotated to follow the sun and its path in the sky.

The most noted singers and dancers of the time visited Edison's studio to perform before the cameras. Famous actors and boxers also appeared in his films.

"Gentleman" Jim Corbett was one of the boxers. Corbett had won the world's heavyweight

Edison built the first motion picture studio at the site of his West Orange labs. Called Black Maria, the building could be rotated to follow the sun.

championship in 1892. Edison paid him fifty dollars a day to perform. It was hard work. Corbett called the studio "the hottest, most cramped place I have ever known."

Edward S. Porter worked for Edison as a film director. He produced *The Great Train Robbery* at Edison's studio. A Western, it was the first film to have a plot. Scenes were linked together to form a story.

The Great Train Robbery was released in December 1903. Like other films of the day, it was only about ten minutes in length. Still, it was a huge success. It led to other story films. To show them, movie theaters opened up by the hundreds all over the country.

The actual making of films did not interest Edison. He left that to others. He put his mind to improving movie cameras and projectors.

Edison also sought to make movies that talked. He kept trying to merge the Kinetoscope with the phonograph. Talking pictures would be the result.

He introduced one of the first talking movie systems at a New York theater in 1913. But it was too complicated to be successful.

The movies would not learn to talk until the late 1920s. By that time, Edison had moved on to other projects.

Edison predicted greatness for the movies. "[Their] greatest mission," he said, "is ... to make people happy... to bring more joy and cheer into this world."

He believed motion pictures "would revolutionize our educational system." Movies would replace textbooks, he believed.

Edison left his mark on the movie industry. He made the first workable movie camera. His Kinetoscope was the first system for viewing motion pictures. He headed one of the nation's foremost movie companies. He is rightly called the "father of motion pictures."

MORE EXPERIMENTS

IN 1907, EDISON CELEBRATED HIS sixtieth birthday. His thick hair had become white. His hearing loss had grown worse.

Yet Edison was still the guiding force at the West Orange labs. He walked through the labs daily to check on the progress of his workers. Francis Upton, who had worked at Menlo Park, said that Edison provided "a constant flow of ideas."

Edison kept control there, but gave workers a free hand in their attempts to solve problems. A new employee once asked Edison about rules. "There are no rules around here," Tom declared. "We're trying to accomplish something."

Despite his age, there were still times that

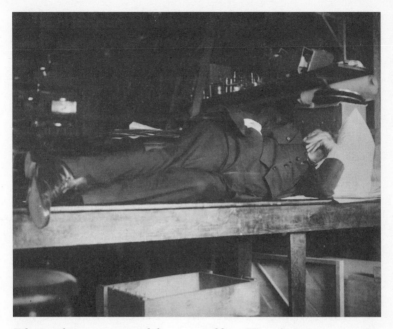

Edison taking a nap on a laboratory table at West Orange.

Edison worked hard and long hours. He worked while most Americans were sleeping. When there was a problem to be solved, he urged assistants to work with him through the night.

At West Orange, every midnight there was a changeover in the power plant, and the lights would go off. It would be dark for a few moments. During the time that the lab was in darkness, Edison would rest his chin on his chest and close his eyes. He would make believe he was in a deep sleep. When the lights went on again, he would pretend to suddenly wake up.

"Well, boys," he would say, "we've had a fine rest. Now let's pitch into work again."

The early 1900s were an exciting time in American social history. The Automobile Age was dawning. Thousands of Americans were steering their horseless carriages along country roads and down city streets.

To Edison, the great value of the automobile was that it woke up Americans. "It has caused them to move, to stir themselves, to get out and away..." he said.

Not all cars of the early 1900s were powered with gasoline engines. Some were steam cars. Others were electric. Electric cars get their power from storage batteries. A storage battery is one that can be recharged. Recharging restores the battery's energy.

Early in the history of automobiles, electric cars were very popular. In 1900, thirty-eight percent of all cars were battery powered. Edison believed that the future belonged to electric cars. They were quiet and easy to drive. They had none of the smelly fumes of the gasoline engine.

As for steam engines, they were costly. And it took a long time to get a steam-powered car going.

But electric cars had their failings, too. Storage batteries of the day wore out quickly, and had to be recharged after about fifty miles of use. There were no long trips in electric cars. The batteries also didn't generate very much power. Few electric cars could travel faster than twenty miles an hour.

Edison took up the challenge of developing a better storage battery. He introduced his first battery in 1904. It was a nickel-iron battery. Edison announced it would lead to "... an automobile for every family."

Edison and his son Theodore posing in a battery-powered automobile.

Some newspapers agreed with him. They said that Edison had "revolutionized the world of power." They said he had triggered "the age of stored electricity."

It didn't happen. The first people to use Edison's batteries got poor results. The battery containers leaked and the batteries themselves went dead after a few months of use.

Edison had to admit his storage battery was a failure. He allowed people to return the bad batteries.

Then he went back to work to make his batteries better. Months went by with little progress. One day, a friend of Tom's visited the lab. He had not seen Edison for many months. He asked Edison whether he was making any headway with the battery project.

Edison flashed a smile. "I've got a lot of results," he said. "I know several hundred things that *won't* work."

The work went on for years. A rugged and more reliable battery was the result. It boasted a longer life than earlier storage batteries.

"At last the battery is finished," Edison wrote in

1909. The next year, Edison's factory began turning out the improved batteries by the hundreds of thousands.

But the demand was never what Edison hoped for. By 1909, the gasoline engine had been found to be superior. Gasoline-powered cars were lower in price. They were more dependable and traveled faster. The popularity of battery-powered cars had nose-dived.

Henry Ford helped to trigger the popularity of gasoline-powered cars. His Ford Motor Company produced the first cars that large numbers of people could afford. In later years, Edison and Ford became close friends.

As soon as Edison saw that the electric car had a dim future, he began to seek other uses for his new storage battery. He was soon selling batteries to power miners' lamps and railroad signal systems. Batteries were used for lighthouses and mountaintop airplane beacons. Storage batteries became one of Edison's best-selling products.

The storage battery wasn't Edison's only interest during the early 1900s. He continued to work to

Edison, his wife, and family at their Glenmont home. From left: daughter Madeleine, Edison's wife Mina, sons Theodore and Charles, and Thomas Edison.

improve the phonograph. He was also deeply involved in the motion picture business. In 1907, he spent $100,000 to build a modern movie studio in the Bronx, a borough of New York City.

Edison's last important experiment involved an unlikely product—rubber. Thanks to the popularity of the rubber-tired automobile, there was a booming demand for rubber.

Rubber trees grow in remote tropical regions. When war broke out in Europe in 1914, and enemy navies threatened to gain control of the sea lanes, America's supply of rubber was threatened. Henry Ford explained the problem to Edison. He asked him to create a new source for rubber.

"I will," Edison said, "some day."

It wasn't until the late 1920s that Edison got around to serious research on rubber. He began by reading all he could about rubber. He started growing hundreds of plant specimens.

"Everything has turned to rubber in our family," said Mrs. Edison. "We talk rubber, think rubber, dream rubber."

Years before, Tom had built a winter home in the little Florida town of Fort Myers. He carried out his rubber research there. He set aside nine acres of his Fort Myers property for growing a variety of vines, plants, and shrubs. One of these, he hoped, would become a good rubber producer.

By 1929, Edison had settled upon the goldenrod as the plant with the greatest chance of success. The rubber in the yellow-flowered goldenrod was, Edison wrote, "entirely in the leaf." Edison invented a machine for stripping the leaves from the plant stem. But the rubber from the goldenrod was not as good as that from the tropics, and it was more expensive to produce.

Edison was nearing his eightieth birthday at this time. His health was failing. Still, he continued his rubber research. "Give me five years," he said, "and the United States will have a rubber crop."

Edison did not get five years. Death was to overtake him before he could finish his work.

CHAPTER 14

THOMAS EDISON
REMEMBERED

O CTOBER 21, 1929, WAS A SPECIAL day. The nation celebrated the fiftieth anniversary of the electric light. "Lights Golden Jubilee" it was called.

Greenfield Village in Dearborn, Michigan, was the center of attention that day. There, Henry Ford had sought to reconstruct early America. A log cabin, a little red schoolhouse, the courtroom where Abraham Lincoln had practiced law, and Patrick Henry's home from Redhill, Virginia, were among the dozens of buildings that Ford had bought and moved to Greenfield Village.

As a tribute to his friend Thomas Edison, Ford devoted a section of Greenfield Village to Menlo

Park. The remains of Edison's two-story wood-frame laboratory had been recovered and shipped to Greenfield Village. A perfect copy of the lab was then constructed.

The "little glass house" where the first lamps were blown was also rebuilt. The boardinghouse where Edison's workers lived was taken apart board by board. It was then put back together at Greenfield Village.

Carloads of red clay from the grounds of the original Menlo Park site were shipped to Greenfield Village, too. Nothing was overlooked. Ford even removed the stump of an old hickory tree that once grew near the laboratory. It was replanted in the village.

Two days before the Jubilee celebration, Thomas and Mina arrived by train at Dearborn. The summer before, the eighty-two-year-old inventor had been seriously ill. His skin was very pale. He walked with a cane.

Henry Ford took the Edisons on a tour of the "new" Menlo Park. After they had inspected the laboratory, Ford asked Edison what he thought.

"Well, you've got this just about ninety-nine and one-half percent perfect," Edison said.

"What is the matter with the other one-half percent?" Ford asked.

"Well, we never kept it as clean as this," Edison answered.

Edison was the star attraction of a huge banquet that was held that evening. As a feature of the evening, he was to light a copy of the first carbon-filament lamp.

An international radio network broadcast the ceremonies. In an excited voice, the radio announcer asked, "Will it light? Will it burn? Or will it flicker and die?"

Edison had two wires in his hand. He made the connection.

"It lights!" cried the announcer.

President Herbert Hoover addressed the banquet guests. Edison spoke next. His voice was faint. He said, "In honoring me you are also honoring that vast army of thinkers and workers without whom my work would have gone for nothing."

At Greenfield Village in Dearborn, Michigan, on October 21, 1929, Edison recreated the experiment that led to the first successful electric light. Looking on are Henry Ford (left) and Francis Jehl, a onetime Edison assistant.

Afterward, Edison slumped in his chair. He turned deathly pale. EDISON COLLAPSES AT JUBILEE, a newspaper headline announced the next day.

Back home at Glenmont, Edison's health continued to fail. His illnesses included diabetes and stomach ulcers, "I am long on ideas but short on time," he said.

He continued to be interested in his rubber research. He seldom went to the laboratory, however. Assistants brought him daily reports of their progress.

By the fall of 1931, Edison was spending most of his time in bed. He was barely able to eat.

Edison sank into a coma on October 14, 1931. He died early in the morning of October 18. He was eighty-four years old.

Mrs. Edison arranged for his body to be viewed at the West Orange laboratory. Thousands came to pay their respects.

Funeral services were held on October 21. President Hoover honored Edison in a unique way. He proposed that on the evening of Edison's funeral that lights all across America be dimmed for a few moments. Thousands of homes and offices carried out the president's suggestion.

Many nations of the world paid tribute to Edison during his lifetime. Italy made him a Grand Officer of the Crown of Italy. France named him a Commander of the French Legion of Honor. The U.S. Congress awarded him with the Congressional Medal of Honor in 1928. Edison once said that he could count his medals by the quart.

At the time of his death, words of praise poured in from people in every part of the world. A New York newspaper called him the "Inventor of the Age." Scores of monuments and memorials would be erected in his honor.

On April 1, 1928, some three years before his death, *The New York Graphic* carried a story about Edison. The headline read: EDISON INVENTS A MACHINE THAT WILL FEED THE HUMAN RACE.

The story and the headline were an April Fool's Day joke. But some people didn't see it as a funny story. They thought it was true.

Edison was, after all, the wizard of electricity. His inventions had changed the face of the world. Feeding the human race was not thought to be beyond his powers. Some people thought that Thomas Edison could do almost anything.

CHRONOLOGY

1847 (February 11) Thomas Alva Edison is born in
      Milan, Ohio.

1854 Family moves to Port Huron, Michigan.

1859 Works as a train boy on the Grand Trunk Railway.

1863 Works as a telegraph operator.

1868 Receives first patent for electric vote recorder.

1871 Marries Mary Stillwell.

1874 Invents quadruplex telegraph.

1876 Establishes laboratory at Menlo Park, New Jersey.

1877 Invents the carbon-button telephone transmitter
      and the phonograph.

1879 Invents the electric lightbulb.

1882 Pearl Street generating plant begins operation.

1884 Wife Mary dies.

1886 Marries Mina Miller.

1887 Opens new laboratory at West Orange, New Jersey.

1889 Develops kinetograph and Kinetoscope.

1894 Demonstrates motion picture machine to the
      public.

1899 Begins work on storage battery.

1909 Develops a practical storage battery.

1927 Begins experiments to make rubber out of
      goldenrod.

1928 Awarded Congressional Medal of Honor.

1931 (October 18) Thomas Alva Edison dies in West
      Orange, New Jersey.

BIBLIOGRAPHY

Primary Sources

Dyer, Frank and Martin, T.C. with William Meadowcroft. *Edison: His Life and Inventions*. New York: Harper Brothers, 1929.

The Diary and Observations of Thomas Alva Edison. Runes, Dagobert D., Editor. New York: Philosophical Library, 1976.

The Papers of Thomas A. Edison. Baltimore: Johns Hopkins University Press.

Volume 1 (1989), *The Making of an Inventor, February 1847– June 1873*.

Volume 2 (1991), *From Laboratory to Workshop, June 1873– March 1876*.

Volume 3 (1995), *Menlo Park, The Early Years, April 1876– December 1877*.

Volume 4 (1998), *The Wizard of Menlo Park, 1878*.

Secondary Sources

Baldwin, Neil. *Inventing the Century*. New York: Hyperion, 1995.

Israel, Paul. *Edison: A Life of Invention*. New York: John Wiley, 1998.

Josephson, Matthew. *Edison: A Biography*. New York: John Wiley, 1992.

Wachhorst, Wyn. *Thomas Alva Edison: An American Myth*. Cambridge, Massachusetts: MIT Press, 1981.

FURTHER READING

Adair, Gene. *Thomas Alva Edison: Inventing the Electric Age*. New York: Oxford University Press, 1996.

Adler, David A. *A Picture Book of Thomas Alva Edison*. New York: Holiday House, 1996.

Anderson, Kelly C. *The Importance of Thomas Edison*. San Diego: Lucent Books, 1994.

Cousins, Margaret. *The Story of Thomas Alva Edison*. New York: Random House (Landmark Books), 1993.

Egan, Louise. *Thomas Edison: The Great American Inventor*. Hauppauge, New York: Barrons Educational, 1987.

FOR MORE INFORMATION

Edison National Historic Site
West Orange, New Jersey
Request brochures titled "Edison" and "Glenmont."
(Main Street and Lakeside Ave., West Orange, NJ 07052)
Phone: (973) 736-0550
Web site: www.nps.gov/edis

Edison Winter Home
Fort Myers, Florida
Request a brochure titled "Edison Winter Home."
(2350 McGregor Blvd., Ft. Myers, FL 33901)

Edison Birthplace Museum
Milan, Ohio
Request brochure titled "Birthplace of Thomas Alva Edison."
(9 Edison Drive, Milan, OH 44846)
Phone: (419) 499-2135
Web site: www.tomedison.org

Henry Ford Museum & Greenfield Village
Dearborn, Michigan
Request brochures titled "Greenfield Village Map" and "Henry Ford Museum Visitor's Guide."
(20900 Oakwood Blvd., Dearborn, MI 48124-4088)
Phone: (313) 271-1620
Web site: www.hfmgv.org

Thomas Edison House
Louisville, Kentucky
(729–731 East Washington, Louisville, KY 40202)
Phone: (502) 585-5247
Web site: www.edison@edisonhouse.com

Note: For a complete rundown on the notebooks, patent materials, business records, and other documents relating to Thomas Edison that have been organized and published by Rutgers University, visit this Web site:
edison.rutgers.edu/

Note: For a state-by-state (or province-by-province) listing of libraries, colleges, historical societies, and other institutions where primary sources are to be found, visit this Web site:
www.uidaho.edu/special-collections/east2html

ACKNOWLEDGMENTS

Many people helped me by providing background information and photographs to be used in this book. Special thanks are due the archivists, curators, photograph specialists, and other staff members at the Edison National Historic Site, West Orange, New Jersey. These include Superintendent Maryanne Gerbaukas; Leonard DeGraaf, Archivist; Beth Aukstikalnis, Curator of Glenmont; Douglas Tarr, Archivist; Ed Wirth, Archivist; and John Warren, Park Ranger. Special thanks are also due Cathleen Latendresse, Manager, Access Services, Henry Ford Museum and Greenfield Village Research Center, Dearborn, Michigan; and Maja Keech, Division of Prints and Photographs, Library of Congress.

George Sullivan, New York City

PHOTO CREDITS

Edison National Historic Site: 7, 9, 15, 18 (left), 18 (right), 23, 45, 51, 54, 56, 58, 60, 63, 67, 70, 72, 73, 77, 79, 85, 86, 89, 92, 95, 99, 102, 103, 107, 112, 118; Library of Congress: 13, 25, 37, 109; Henry Ford Museum/Greenfield Village: 27, 35, 39; Morsecode.com: 32; New York Public Library: 46, 61; *Photography in America* by William Welling: 101

INDEX

Bold numbers refer to photographs